Smithsonian

BIRD DETECTIVES

SCIENCE SLEUTHS AND THEIR FEATHERED FRIENDS

BY KRISTINE RIVERS AND CARLA J. DOVE

CAPSTONE PRESS
a capstone imprint

Published by Capstone Press, an imprint of Capstone
1710 Roe Crest Drive, North Mankato, Minnesota 56003
capstonepub.com

Library of Congress Cataloging-in-Publication Data is available on the Library of Congress website.

ISBN: 9781669010968 (hardcover)
ISBN: 9781669040255 (paperback)
ISBN: 9781669010920 (ebook PDF)

Summary: Discover the fascinating work of bird detectives from the Smithsonian Institution and the Division of Birds at the National Museum of Natural History. These avian experts use science and technology to study clues—like feather characteristics and where birds are found—to solve bird mysteries. One of the most important areas of their research involves identifying species of birds that collide with aircraft, known as bird strikes. Their research findings help improve aviation safety to keep birds and people safe. Jam-packed with behind-the-scenes photos, fun facts, and an interactive case study, this book is sure to fascinate bird enthusiasts, young and old.

Editor: Donald Lemke; Designer: Sarah Bennett; Media Researcher: Svetlana Zhurkin; Production Specialist: Katy LaVigne

Our very special thanks to Kealy Gordon, Product Development Manager, and the following at Smithsonian Enterprises: Jill Corcoran, Director, Licensed Publishing; Brigid Ferraro, Vice President, Education and Consumer Products; and Carol LeBlanc, President, Smithsonian Enterprises.

Image Credits
Alamy: TNS/Chicago Tribune/John Bordsen, 5 (top); Associated Press: File/Bebeto Matthews, 5 (bottom); CDC: Janice Haney Carr, 15 (bottom left); Getty Images: AFP/Yuri Cortez, 24, Bloomberg/Andrew Harrer, 11 (top), Daniel Grill, 9 (bottom), Fanny Boyer, 11 (bottom), 25 (footprint inset), imageBROKER/Lilly, 23, Science Photo Library/Tek Image, 20; James Kegley: cover (bottom middle), 9 (top), 12 (top), 14, 21; Shutterstock: Anghi, cover (top), Aves y estrellas, 18 (bottom left), Boonchuay Promjiam, 12 (middle left), Daniil Skoblov, 3, David Smart, 18–19 (folder background), David Spates, back cover (bottom), Elizaveta Galitckaia, 15 (top), Eric Isselee, 19 (bottom), Evgeniy Yatskov, cover (middle right), FotoRequest, 25 (back and bird's feet inset), 27, Gallinago_media, 12 (bottom right), HorenkO, 18–19 (background texture), Just2shutter (paper with folded corner), 7, 11, 13, 17, 21, 25, little birdie, 13, 25 (feather inset), Ludmila Kapustkina, 12 (bottom left), MartaPo, 29, Matt Binding, 18 (bottom right), MaxFX, 22, Michael O'Keene, 4, Mike Truchon, 31, Mikhail Balashov, 18 (top), MoreVector, 19 (top), muratart, back cover (top), mycteria (feather), cover (middle), 1 (top), nadtytok, 12 (middle right), Nena Ray, 26, Netkoff (magnifying glass), cover and throughout, Paul Reeves Photography, 23 (inset), Protasov AN, 30 (bottom), stuar, 8 (soap bottle), Vadim Petrakov, 1, Vector Tradition (bird footprints), cover and throughout, Wanida_Sri, 28, Yuriy Kostin, 8 (bubbles); Smithsonian Institution Archives: 6, 10, 17 (bottom), 25 (SEM inset); Smithsonian Institution: Carla J. Dove, cover (bottom left and right), 15 (bottom right), 16, 18 (middle, both), 19 (middle), Lisa Bailey, 17 (nodal shapes), National Museum of Natural History, 7, 8 (top)

TABLE OF CONTENTS

BIRDS AND HUMANS COLLIDE

Throughout history, birds and humans have been closely connected. Long ago, early peoples trailed birds to fresh water. Voyagers followed birds to find land. Birds even inspired people to fly and helped make that feat possible.

But as people took to the skies, interactions between birds and humans became more common—and riskier for both birds and humans.

By the 1950s, airplanes started becoming a popular form of transportation. At the same time, collisions between planes and birds increased. These **bird strikes**, as they are called, sometimes damaged aircraft. They also put people and birds in danger.

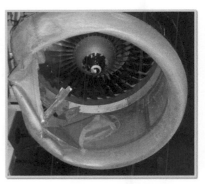

A jet engine damaged by a bird strike

Something needed to change.

To help reduce the risk of these events, the U.S. military and the Federal Aviation Administration in the United States began collecting samples from bird strikes. They sent these samples to the Division of Birds at the Smithsonian's National Museum of Natural History. The researchers who would study these small, charred bird remains became known as . . . bird detectives.

In 2009, US Airways flight 1549 was forced to land in the Hudson River near New York City after a bird strike. Bird detectives at the Smithsonian Institution used remains found in the jet's engines to identify the birds involved in the accident as Canada geese.

THE FIRST BIRD DETECTIVE

The job of bird detective did not always exist. This job was first created by Roxie Collie Laybourne (1910–2003), an aide in the Division of Birds at the Smithsonian's National Museum of Natural History. When Laybourne began working at the museum, most of the jobs were occupied by men. But she was perfect for this difficult task. She was skilled at animal **taxidermy** and was interested in airplane mechanics.

Roxie Collie Laybourne studying museum specimens in the 1960s

Laybourne, who later became known as the "Feather Detective," pioneered **forensic** ornithology. She used scientific methods to study **evidence** and identify bird **species**. With microscopes and museum specimens, Laybourne was able to figure out the types of birds involved in bird-aircraft collisions. She even helped solve criminal investigations for government agencies—including the FBI—by identifying feathers found at crime scenes.

Modern bird detectives follow in Laybourne's footsteps. Carla Dove, Program Director at the Smithsonian's Feather Identification Lab in the Division of Birds, and her research team still identify species of birds from very small samples. They use clues—such as microscopic differences in the feathers and

Laybourne (left) and Carla Dove study the remains of a bird strike.

DNA—to study birds and help us understand these types of human-wildlife conflicts. Their work is critical to preventing future bird strikes.

FOLLOW THE TRAIL

THE CASE OF THE MYSTERY BIRD

An unknown bird has collided with a small plane—and you are a bird detective! Search for more "Follow the Trail" boxes throughout this book. Use the clues in each box to help identify what species of bird was involved in this bird strike.

COLLECTING AND COMPARING

Today, bird detectives at Smithsonian's Feather Identification Lab receive thousands of feather samples, mainly from bird-strike events. In fact, the lab receives around 40 samples every day. That's more than 10,000 samples per year!

A sample of Northern Flicker feathers found on an airport runway

Not all feather samples come from bird strikes. Bird detectives work to identify samples from other types of bird studies too. They include samples from **invasive** species studies to examine what birds are eaten by non-native animals. Bird detectives also study samples from anthropological artifacts. This helps us understand which birds were important to early cultures.

No matter the case, bird detectives treat every sample with care. Sometimes they need to gently clean the sample feathers with soapy water.

Samples containing whole feathers are very useful. Bird detectives are able to study each feather's overall appearance, or **morphology**. They look for clues such as size, color, shape, pattern, and texture.

These clues help bird detectives figure out where the feather came from on the bird's body. Did the feather come from a wing? Did it come from a tail? Knowing this information helps bird detectives narrow their search for the exact species.

Researcher Sarah Luttrell matches tail feathers to a museum specimen of American Kestrel.

🐦 A LITTLE BIRD TOLD ME: FEATHERS AND THE LAW

If you find a feather, study it. But then return it to nature! Did you know a permit is required to keep any part of most birds? This includes feathers lost naturally, or **molted**. Laws help prevent people from illegally hunting wild birds for their beautiful feathers or meat.

SMITHSONIAN COLLECTIONS

Bird detectives use a variety of techniques to figure out what types of birds are included with each feather sample. They check the possible types of birds against illustrations and photographs in field guides. They study range maps showing the seasonal locations of certain bird species. But perhaps the most important step is comparing feather samples to the bird **specimens** found in the Smithsonian's Division of Birds.

Laybourne and other scientists stand among the collection of bird specimens at the Smithsonian's Division of Birds.

This isn't just any ordinary specimen collection—it's one of the largest collections of bird specimens in the world! The massive collection includes bird skeletons and skins. It includes eggs, nests, and much more. Many of these specimens are hundreds of years old!

The Smithsonian collection houses birds from around the world. About 85% of the nearly 10,000 known bird species are included in the collection.

Study skins (specimens) like these Laughing Gulls are stored in drawers to preserve them for long-term studies.

Researchers maintain the fragile bird specimens within a series of cabinet drawers. The drawers are organized by **Order** and **Family** of birds. Scientists recognize more than 40 Orders of birds and more than 240 bird families.

FOLLOW THE TRAIL

MYSTERY BIRD TRACKS

The mystery bird left footprints near the bird-strike event. Study the photograph for clues! The bird has a large foot, measuring about 4 inches (10 centimeters) in length. How many toes do you count? Can you rule out any species of birds yet?

THE FEATHER EXPERTS

In order to compare feather samples to their collection of specimens, bird detectives must be feather experts. They know feathers provide many clues about the species of bird that they belong to. Feathers are like a bird's fingerprints!

Jim Whatton and Faridah Dahlan examine a museum specimen of a Great Horned Owl.

In fact, birds are the only living creatures with feathers. They keep birds warm and dry. They shape their bodies. They give birds the ability to fly. Feathers also provide color for display and **camouflage**. Feathers come in an amazing variety of colors, shapes, sizes, and textures.

PARTS OF A FEATHER

Every feather is made up of many different parts, and bird detectives must know them all. Knowing the parts of a feather helps bird detectives identify which birds the feathers came from.

Study the key parts of a feather for yourself:

rachis—the feather's main shaft; it has many rows of tiny strands, or barbs, attached to it.

pennaceous barbs—branching from the feather's shaft, like limbs on a tree. This type of barb has hooklets that help form the feather shape.

plumulaceous barbs—the downy or fluffy barbs found near the base of a feather. Barbules branch from downy barbs and have microscopic clues that bird detectives rely on for study.

vane—the smooth, flat part of a feather

calamus—the hollow tube at the base of the feather, sometimes called the quill

FOLLOW THE TRAIL

MYSTERY BIRD FEATHER

The feather above is from the mystery bird! Investigators found it associated with the bird strike. Study all of its parts. Does this feather look like one you've seen before? If not, don't worry! Search for more clues in the pages ahead.

A DETECTIVE'S TOOLS

Although all birds have feathers, bird detectives are trained to spot small differences among the feathers of different species of birds. Many times, these differences aren't visible to the naked eye. Thankfully, bird detectives have the technology to view **microscopic** details.

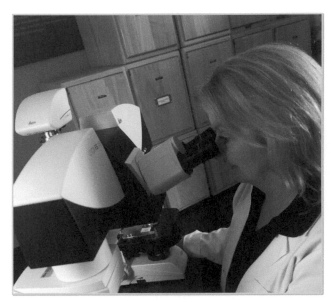

Bird detective Carla Dove views feather barbs with a light microscope.

Bird detectives use many high-tech tools in their mystery-solving research. The Feather Identification Lab has state-of-the-art magnification tools to examine samples. Researchers use microscopes to study the smallest parts of a feather. First, they remove a few downy feather barbs. Then, they mount these barbs on a microslide to study the features.

Light microscopes allow researchers to see tiny features within the downy barbules, such as **pigment**, node shape, and barbule length. Bird detectives search for microscopic features that are found in specific groups or Orders of birds.

The research team may also use a scanning electron microscope (SEM). This type of microscope is incredibly powerful. SEMs can magnify a feather sample by more than 1,000 times!

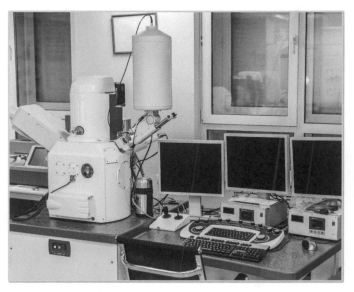

Scanning electron microscope

Compare the SEM micrographs below. If you were a bird detective, do you think you could tell the two types of barbs apart?

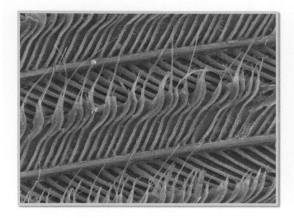

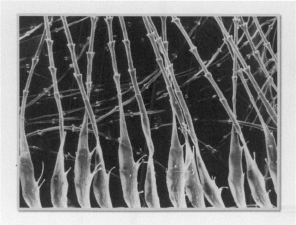

The **pennaceous barb** found on the smooth part of the feather vane has clearly visible hooklets that attach to the barbules next to them.

The **plumulaceous barb** from the fluffy part of the feather has barbules with distinct nodal features (see p.17).

DOWNY FEATHER STRUCTURES

A very important way bird detectives identify birds from feathers is by looking at the nodal structures found in the downy barbules. These microscopic structures are located where cells join along the strands of downy barbules.

The function of nodal structures remains a mystery to bird detectives and other **ornithologists**. Maybe they prevent feather tangling. Maybe they trap air close to a bird's body for warmth. It's still being studied.

However, researchers do know that the nodal structures of many bird groups have unique shapes. These structures provide important clues to identify the group or Order of birds in which the mystery species belongs. This helps narrow identification possibilities.

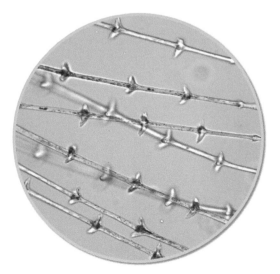

The microscopic structures of a downy feather offer clues to the type of bird it belongs to. These star-like nodal structures are typical of birds in the dove Family.

Some examples of the downy barbule nodal shapes of common bird Orders:

Galliformes have ring-shaped structures at the nodes; this group includes chickens, turkeys, and other fowl-like birds.

Anseriformes have triangular nodes; this group of birds includes geese, ducks, and other waterfowl.

Columbiformes have star- or flower-shaped nodes; this group of birds includes pigeons and doves.

Accipitriformes have prong-shaped nodes; this group includes birds of prey, like eagles and hawks.

MYSTERY BIRD NODES

The mystery bird's downy feather has ring-shaped nodes. Does the mystery bird's nodal structure (shown at right) match any of the structures above? You're getting closer to identifying the mystery bird!

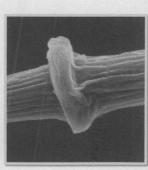

FOLLOW THE TRAIL

THE VIKING PILLOW MYSTERY

The Smithsonian's Feather Identification Lab once received samples from a feather pillow—but not just *any* pillow! It was discovered in an ancient Viking boat grave in a Norwegian bog. The pillow dated back to AD 800–1050. That's about 1,000 years old!

Sample of the pillow stuffing found in a Viking boat grave

Lab Program Director Carla Dove and her colleagues in Norway worked together to study the brittle samples for microscopic clues. They spotted triangular nodes that are unique to ducks, geese, and swans. These birds are members of the Order Anseriformes.

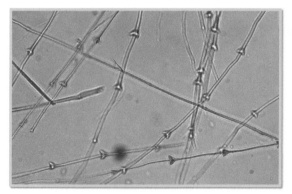

Downy feather barbules viewed through a microscope. Notice the triangular-shaped nodes that are features of waterfowl.

Great Cormorant

King Eider

A feather from the Viking pillow is matched to a specimen of a Great Cormorant. The feather at the forceps matches perfectly with the feathers of the museum specimen.

After additional research, the team determined that the feathers of three Families were used as pillow stuffing: eiders, cormorants, and gulls.

Herring Gull

SOLVING MYSTERIES WITH DNA

Bird detectives sometimes identify birds from very small samples. As you might imagine, when aircraft and birds collide there isn't much left of the bird. Bird-strike samples may contain nothing more than a mixture of feather fragments, blood, tissue, and fat. This mixture is known as **snarge**.

Researchers at the Feather Identification Lab sometimes rely on yet another research tool to solve cases that have minute samples: DNA. The team's genetic specialist works to extract short DNA sequences called DNA barcodes. The unknown sequences are then compared to a library of known bird barcodes. Unlike microscopy, this method may provide identification to the species level. The team confirms accuracy by checking range maps to ensure the identified species occurs in the area where and when the bird strike occurred.

DNA samples are placed in vials like this.

Even this method isn't fail-proof! Sometimes the snarge is too degraded to yield a DNA sequence, or the material has been contaminated. Using feather clues is then the only tool available. In most cases, the team studies feather and DNA clues together, confirming species identification using multiple lines of evidence.

Researcher Faridah Dahlan studies a snarge sample.

Although snarge may be gross, accurately identifying species involved in bird strikes is the most important role of the Feather Identification Lab. Knowing the bird species that live in and around an airfield gives insight into the bird's lifestyle and habits. This is key information needed to develop solutions to prevent future collisions.

FOLLOW THE TRAIL

MYSTERY BIRD LOCATION

The bird-strike event you're investigating took place near a forest of oak trees, with fields or agricultural land nearby. Can you think of any birds that might live in this type of location? Have you figured out the mystery bird's identity yet?

DEVELOPING SOLUTIONS

Bird strikes cause billions of dollars in damage every year. Most bird strikes happen during airplane takeoffs and landings. Keeping birds away from airfields lowers repair costs and helps save birds!

This is not as easy as it sounds. Over time, a species may move from one area to another. There may be more birds from one year to the next. Each airfield needs its own custom-made plans to prevent bird strikes. That's why the detective work done by the Feather Identification Lab is so important.

A sign to discourage feeding birds near an airport

Bird detectives at the Feather Identification Lab always keep a close eye on bird-strike data. That's because knowledge is ever-evolving as bird populations change over time. Their research has led to many important changes.

AIRFIELD BIOLOGISTS

Scientists known as airfield **biologists** work at every major airport. They focus on wildlife and habitat management to prevent bird strikes. To do this, airfield biologists must understand where the impacted birds live and where they travel. They study what the birds eat, how they feed, and where they rest. This helps them develop habitat and wildlife management plans that prevent bird strikes and keep the skies safe for all who fly!

🐤 A LITTLE BIRD TOLD ME: BARN SWALLOWS AND BIRD STRIKES

What birds are often involved in bird strikes? Barn swallows! Barn swallows have a wide range, living all over the world. The birds fly in flocks and feed on insects over open areas, such as airfields. This behavior puts them at risk.

Today, airfield biologists have many ways to help keep birds away. They fire loud propane cannons to warn birds of potential danger. They use trained dogs to chase off large birds, such as geese. They even broadcast **predator** calls over loudspeakers!

Airport managers may change the landscape to be less bird-friendly. They change the type and height of grasses used. They fill in ponds so birds are attracted to areas away from airfields. Other times, they'll trap birds and move them to a safer location. This work helps make air travel safe. Today, air travel remains the safest way to journey over long distances.

An airport dog chases birds from a runway.

FOLLOW the TRAIL

MYSTERY BIRD CLUES

You've gathered all the clues about the mystery bird! Study the information you found. Can you guess what type of bird left these clues behind?

☐ The mystery bird left tracks by walking on the ground.

☐ The mystery bird has a large foot, measuring about 4 inches (10 cm) in length.

☐ The mystery bird has three toes facing forward and one facing backward.

☐ A large feather measuring about 1 foot (0.3 meters) in length was found associated with the bird-strike event.

☐ The mystery bird feather is patterned with barring: thick, rusty-colored stripes separated by dark brown stripes.

☐ The mystery bird's plumulaceous barbules, from the downy part of the feather, have ring-shaped nodal structures.

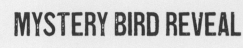

FOLLOW THE TRAIL

MYSTERY BIRD REVEAL

It's time to solve the case of the mystery bird . . .

If you guessed **WILD TURKEY**, you're correct!

This large, heavy ground bird spends most of its time in open woodlands, clearings, and fields searching for acorns, nuts, seeds, and berries. The huge tail feathers have dark brown or black and rusty-colored barring. As in all members of the wildfowl Family, the plumulaceous feather barbules have ring-shaped nodal structures. Nice work!

Although wild turkeys can't fly very high in the air, they are sometimes involved in bird strikes because most of these happen near ground-level during takeoff and landing. Which methods do you think would be most effective to keep them away from airfields?

FUTURE BIRD DETECTIVES

In the years ahead, the work of bird detectives will become even more important. As new types of aircraft fill the sky—including drones and airborne vehicles—human-wildlife conflicts are sure to increase. But, with the help of detectives and airport biologists, the airways can remain safe for birds and humans alike.

BECOME A SCIENTIST

Bird detectives are only one kind of scientist. As you grow older, volunteering your time is one of the best ways to learn about any field of science, including ornithology. Many organizations offer internships, which provide great opportunities to try out different types of work while supporting everyday operational needs. For example, Smithsonian volunteers assist staff in caring for collections, gathering research data, program administration, and other critical functions.

For now, check out your local nature center or look for Smithsonian online programs. Volunteer with feeding or cleaning duties at a nearby bird rescue organization. Join in citizen science efforts such as bird counts and nest watches.

COURSEWORK AND CAREER PATHS

If you plan to pursue a career in ornithology or a related field, take courses in biology and other sciences as well as mathematics. Learn as much as you can about birds that live near you. Practice your observation skills and keep notes in a nature journal. A wide variety of career paths within ornithology and biology are out there and are ready to be explored—the sky is the limit!

ABOUT THE AUTHORS

Kristine Rivers is a lifelong birder, author, and the founder of Birding for Fun, an organization offering guided tours, workshops, and family-friendly events meant to make birding accessible to everyone. She is a proud Texas Master Naturalist and served as president of her local chapter. She's written popular field journals, birding activity books, and bird-watching guides for kids.

photo by James Kegley

Carla J. Dove is the Program Manager at the Feather Identification Lab at the Smithsonian Institution's National Museum of Natural History in Washington, D.C. She is an expert in determining species of birds from microscopic evidence, feather comparisons with the museum's specimens, and DNA barcoding. Her lab's work is essential to the field of aviation safety.

GLOSSARY

biologist (bye-AHL-oh-gist)—someone who studies a branch of knowledge that deals with living organisms and life processes

bird strike (BURD STRYK)—a collision involving an aircraft and one or more birds

camouflage (KAM-oh-flaj)—the hiding or disguising of something to make it blend in with the environment

DNA (dee-en-AY)—material in cells that gives birds and almost all other living organisms their individual characteristics; DNA stands for deoxyribonucleic acid.

evidence (EV-uh-duhnss)—material presented to help solve mysteries

Family (FAM-uh-lee)—a group of related plants or animals ranking in biological classification above a genus and below an Order

forensic (fuh-REN-sik)—the application of scientific knowledge to legal problems especially in regard to criminal evidence

invasive (in-VAY-siv)—tending to spread

microscopic (my-kruh-SKAH-pik)—able to be seen only through a microscope

molt (MOHLT)—to shed feathers with the cast-off parts being replaced by a new growth

morphology (mohr-FAHL-uh-jee)—the form and structure of a plant or animal, or the way it looks

Order (ORD-ur)—category of biological classification ranking above the Family and below the class

ornithologist (or-nuh-THOL-uh-jist)—scientist who studies birds

pigment (PIHG-muhnt)—a natural coloring matter in animals and plants

predator (PRED-uh-tuhr)—an animal that lives by preying on and eating other animals

snarge (SNARJ)—remains from a bird strike consisting of a mixture of microscopic feather fragments, blood, and tissue

species (SPEE-sheez)—a group of plants or animals that share common characteristics and are capable of interbreeding

specimen (SPESS-uh-muhn)—a portion of material for use in testing or examination, or a voucher in a museum

taxidermy (TAK-suh-duhr-mee)—the skill or occupation of preparing, stuffing, and mounting skins of animals

INDEX

READ MORE SMITHSONIAN BOOKS!